DIRTY JOKES FOR WOMEN

Liz Hughes

Michael O'Mara Books Limited

This edition published in 1995 by
Michael O'Mara Books Limited
9 Lion Yard, Tremadoc Road
London SW4 7NQ

Copyright © 1995 by
Michael O'Mara Books Limited

All rights reserved. No part of this publication
may be reproduced, stored in a retrieval
system, or transmitted, in any form or by any
means without the prior permission in writing of
the publisher, nor be otherwise circulated in any form
of binding or cover other than that in which it is
published and without a similar condition
including this condition being imposed on
the subsequent purchaser.

A CIP catalogue record for this book is available from
the British Library.

ISBN 1-85479-773-5

Printed and bound by Cox & Wyman, Reading.

10 9 8 7 6 5 4 3 2 1

Him:

'When women look at me they instantly think of sex.'

Her:

'Yeh, cos you look like a prick.'

'Has your husband been circumcised?'

'No, he's a complete dick.'

What goes in dry, comes out wet and gives a lot of satisfaction?

A tea bag.

I went to see a palmist and she told me I'd been single for a long time.

'How do you know that?' I asked.

'Because the tips of the first two fingers on your right hand are so worn down they've lost their print.'

A woman goes back to her new lover's house for the first night and he suggests they try out his pack of flavoured condoms. The lights go out and she goes down on him.

'Ooh great,' she says, 'cheese and onion.'

'Hang on,' he says, 'I haven't got it on yet.'

A woman was in bed with her new boyfriend.

'Darling,' she said, 'how would it be if you came up me from behind?'

'Oh,' he replied, 'wouldn't that be a bit perverted?'

'Perverted!' she said, 'that's a big word for a 12-year-old!'

What's the difference between a hedgehog and an XR3i?

A hedgehog has the pricks on the outside.

◆◀◆

Cinderella wanted to go to the ball and suddenly her fairy godmother appeared.

'Cinderella, you shall go to the ball,' she said.

'But fairy godmother, I have nothing to wear!'

Shazam, there was a beautiful ball dress.

'But fairy godmother, it's the wrong time of the month!'

Shazam, there was a tampon.

'Now remember, you have to be back by midnight,' warned the fairy godmother.

Cinders had a wonderful time at the ball and danced with the Prince all night but as the clock struck 12 she suddenly disappeared.

As the Prince ran after her, all he heard was a blood-curdling scream. The tampon had turned into a pumpkin.

◆ ◆ ◆

What's a virgin sheep?

One that can run faster than an Aussie shepherd.

– | –

Why are Catholic men like British Rail?

They never pull out in time.

– | –

What four-letter word ending in 'k' do men use to mean sex?

Talk.

Her:

> I dreamt of you last night.

Him:

> Did you?

Her:

> No, you wouldn't let me.

A sailor went to see his doctor when he found out his wife was pregnant.

'She can't be pregnant, doc — I've been at sea for the past year.'

The doctor explained that this was a 'grudge pregnancy.'

'What do you mean?' asked the sailor.

'Someone had it in for you,' replied the doctor.

Mummy, what's an orgasm?

'I don't know dear, ask your father.'

☆ ☆ ☆

When is the safest time for sex?

When your boyfriend's away.

If it's true that eight out of ten men write with a ball-point pen, what do the other two do with it?

My doctor's told me I have to give up half my sex life but I can't decide which half to give up — talking about it or thinking about it.

Her:

Let's make love a different way tonight, darling! Let's do it back to back.

Him:

Don't be silly, you can't make love back to back.

Her:

Yes, you can, I've invited the bloke next door.

Hearing agonized screams coming from the outpatients' department, a doctor rushed in and yelled at a student nurse.

'For goodness sake, nurse! I said remove his *spectacles* and prick his *boils*!'

It was a young man's first night and after stripping off in the dark he slipped his willy into the girl's hand.

'What do you think of that?' he asked proudly.

'Oh, thanks very much,' she said, 'but I won't smoke it now, I'll slip it behind my ear for later.'

'**M**ummy, why do fairy tales always start with "Once upon a time . . . "?'

'**T**hey don't always; your father's, for instance, always start with "Bloody train was late again . . . ".'

Woman out on the town talking to her friend:

'Have you ever been picked up by the fuzz?'

'No, but I have been swung by the tits a few times.'

A woman on the phone to her friend:

'That husband of mine's a liar, he says he spent the night with his mate Dave.'

'Well maybe he did,' replied her friend.

'No he didn't. *I* spent the night with Dave.'

◇ ◊ ◇

Two neighbours were praising their new milkman.

'He's very good-looking, punctual and dresses so smartly,' said one.

'Yes, and so quickly too!' replied the other.

☆☆☆

First Woman:

'What do you think of sex on television?'

Second Woman:

'Very uncomfortable.'

What's the only sure way of getting something hard between your legs?

Buying a motorbike.

✖✖✖

What is LXIX?

69 the hard way.

What do sex and bridge have in common? If you don't have a good partner, a good hand will do.

Woman:

The doctor said I have the legs of a 17-year-old!

Man:

Yeh? What did he say about your 65-year-old ass?

Woman:

Oh, he didn't mention you.

Nurse:

Doctor, why is that old man sticking out his tongue and holding up his middle finger?

Doctor:

Because I asked him to show me his sexual organs.

How do you know if your man's bad in bed?

He gives up sex for Lent and you don't notice until Easter.

What do men and dog-mess have in common?

The older they get the easier they are to pick up.

My boyfriend's so bad in bed that when they see him even prostitutes have a headache.

Who's the most popular man
in a nudist camp?

The man who can carry
two cups of coffee and
a dozen doughnuts at the
same time.

– I –

What do you call a man with
no willy?

A sucker.

I've divorced my husband because of illness — I got sick of him.

My man's an animal. He makes love like a penguin

– once a year.

What's pink and hard and comes in the morning?

The FT crossword.

on't stand for
sexual harassment
in the office.
Lie on the desk.

When God gave out brains my husband thought he'd said trains, so he asked for a small, slow one.

What's hairy and has six
sides?

A pubic cube.

What's the difference
between Herpes and
true love?

Herpes lasts forever.

I like blond men best — they get dirty quicker.

— I —

My boyfriend's such an idiot he thinks Van Dyck is a lesbian truck driver.

— I —

Bestiality — 9 out of 10 cats said their owners preferred it.

What's long and hard and
has semen in it?

A submarine.

◆ ◆ ◆

Definition of sex?

One damp thing after
another.

1st Woman:

What would you do if you found that someone was screwing your husband?

2nd Woman:

I'd shoot her guide-dog.

***

Is Muffin the Mule a sexual offence?

No, but Dobbin the Horse might be.

***

☆☆☆

What do you get when you cross a donkey with an onion?

A piece of ass that makes your eyes water.

Him:

I'm really into cloning.

Her:

So, go screw yourself!

Tory ministers are the cream of society — thick, rich and full of clots.

With a boyfriend like mine, who needs enemas?

Lesbianism – when only your breast is good enough.

My boyfriend's so stupid he thinks genitalia is an Italian airline.

Him:

I'm twelve inches long and three inches thick.

Her:

That's fine but how big's your willy?

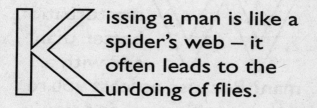

Kissing a man is like a spider's web — it often leads to the undoing of flies.

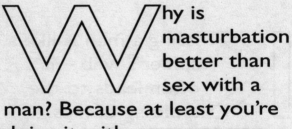hy is masturbation better than sex with a man? Because at least you're doing it with someone you love.

Sex is like a bank account
— after withdrawal you
lose interest.

◆ ◆ ◆

What has 27 teeth and holds
back the Incredible Hulk?

My zipper.

Support women's lib — use his razor.

The bigger they are, the harder they maul.

Underneath every successful man there is a woman.

1st Woman:

Do you like masked balls?

2nd Woman:

No, I like to know who I'm sleeping with.

⊛⊛⊛

What's the best thing about men?

They're such cunning linguists.

Virginity is like a balloon —
one prick and it's gone.

Definition of the lateral
coital position —
having a bit on the side.

If jewelry is a collection of jewels, flattery is a collection of flats and a pantry is a collection of pants, then what is coquetry?

I thought the clap was a form of applause until I met my boyfriend.

***

Support women's lib — make him sleep in the wet patch.

***

Always remember, a 12-inch prick is a rule not an exception.

1st Woman:

Would you say your boyfriend was well hung?

2nd Woman:

Well, put it this way, he buys his socks in threes.

What's a man's definition of a
romantic evening?

Sex.

How are men like blenders?

You know you need one,
but you're not quite
sure why.

A man was trying to chat up an attractive woman in a bar and used his best line.

'Haven't I seen you somewhere before?'

'Yes,' she replied. 'I'm the receptionist at the VD clinic.'

Why can't Santa Claus have babies?

Because he only comes once a year and then it's down the chimney.

✖✖✖

Why should you always be on top when you're in bed with a stupid man?

Because they can only fuck you up.

I went to the gynaecologist the other day and she said,

'You've been married a long time haven't you?'

'Yes, how can you tell?'

'It's almost healed up.'

How do you know if your boyfriend's a wanker?

He shouts his own name when he comes.

Why aren't priests like other men?

Because all children call them father except their own who call them uncle.

Why should you not screw a Porsche driver?

Because they never check to see if you're coming before they pull out.

Him:

Hello, darling, do you come here often?

Her:

Only when I wank.

◆ ◆ ◆

'Mummy, I woke up while I was on the operating table.'

'So? I woke up once while I was making love to your father.'

What's the last thing you'll
find in me?

My husband.

How are men like
Chinese meals?

They satisfy you, but only
for a little while.

How are men and spray-
paint alike?

One squeeze and they're
all over you.

✖✖✖

How do you keep a man
from wanting sex?

Marry him.

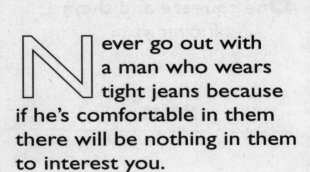

Never go out with a man who wears tight jeans because if he's comfortable in them there will be nothing in them to interest you.

What are the ups and downs of marriage?

The toilet seat is always up and his interest is always down.

◆ ◆ ◆

How are men like microwaves in bed?

30 seconds and they're done.

What's the best way to keep a man happy in bed?

Bring the TV into the bedroom.

Man:

I don't want to wear a
condom tonight — it cuts
down on what I feel.

Woman:

Good, then we'll be even.

Man:

Darling, am I the first man to make love to you?

Woman:

Of course you are, I don't know why you men always ask the same silly question.

Man:

Do you believe in free love?

Woman:

Have I ever given you a bill?

How do you know your man suffers from premature ejaculation?

When he comes walking in the door.

◆ ◆ ◆

What's the difference between worry and panic?

About 28 days.

Definition of paranoia:

putting a condom on your vibrator.

How do you know if you're having a super orgasm?

Your husband wakes up.

Him:

Hey baby, I'd like to get in your pants.

Her:

I don't think so, one arsehole in there's enough.

Husband:

Wanna have a quickie?

Wife:

As opposed to what?

My husband had a terrible accident at the golf course yesterday — he fell off the ball-washer.

Why were men given larger
brains than dogs?

So they wouldn't hump
women's legs at cocktail
parties.

Man:

  Was I your first?

Woman:

  What do you mean *was*?
  Have you already done it?

What do you do if a
Rottweiler starts humping
your leg?

Fake an orgasm.

My ex-husband went
to a premature ejaculators'
meeting but nobody
was there.

He was two hours early!

Husband:

I saw you with a strange man today at lunch. Now I want an explanation and I want the truth.

Wife:

Well, make up your mind. Which do you want?

Why is life like a penis?

Because when it's soft
it's hard to beat,
but when its hard you
get screwed.

What do you call the
area between the vagina
and the anus?

A chin rest.

What goes in hard and stiff
and comes out soft and wet?

Chewing gum.

Men, give them an inch and
they add it to their own.

What do you call sex
with your husband?

Trivial pursuit.

1st Woman:

I wonder how long cocks
should be sucked.

2nd Woman:

Same as short ones.

☆☆☆

A woman went into a shop for some batteries.

'Certainly, come this way,' the shop assistant said.

'If I could come that way,' said the woman, 'I wouldn't need the batteries.'

1st Woman: *(looking at her salary)*

Nowadays my pay is like a handful of hard cock.

2nd Woman:

What do you mean?

1st Woman:

Well, it gives you a good feeling, but it seems like the more you work, the less you have to hold on to.

What would you rather be, a light bulb, or a bowling ball?

It depends if you'd rather be screwed or fingered.

◆ ◆ ◆

The only time my husband wakes up stiff is when he's worked out at the gym the night before.

Why is sex like thin air?

It's no big thing unless you aren't getting any.

Did you hear that they are going to stop circumcising men?

They've discovered they've been throwing away the best part.

What's the difference
between hard and dark?

It stays dark all night.

Do you know why it's
called sex?

Because it's easier
to spell than **Uhhh** . . .
**ohhhh . . . ahhhhh . . .
aieeeeee!**

◆ ◆ ◆

A woman went to the doctor complaining that she was exhausted all the time.

'How many times a week do you have sex?' he asked.

'Every Monday, Wednesday and Saturday,' she replied.

When the doctor suggested she cut out Wednesdays she was horrified.

'I can't, that's the only night I'm home with my husband.'

◆ ◆ ◆

Husband:

If I died, would you get married again?

Wife:

I suppose so.

Husband:

Would you make love to him?

Wife:

He would be my husband, dear.

Husband:

Would you give him my golf clubs?

Wife:

No, he's left-handed.

What do you have when
you have two little green balls
in your hand?

Kermit's undivided attention.

⬤⬤⬤

What's the best thing
to come out of a penis when
you stroke it?

The wrinkles.

✖✖✖

A woman goes into a gun shop to buy a rifle.

'It's for my husband,' she explained.

'Did he tell you what gauge to get?' asked the assistant.

'Certainly not! He doesn't even know I'm going to shoot him!'

Advice for new brides:

1) Tell your husband you have to have one night a week out with the girls.

2) Don't waste it with the girls.

What's the worst thing about giving a man a blow job?

The view.

◆◆◆

'I'm worried,' said the woman to her doctor.

'I found my daughter and the little boy next door naked and examining each other's bodies.'

'That's not unusual,' replied the doctor, 'I wouldn't worry about it.'

'But I am worried,' she said, 'and so is my daughter's husband.'

◆◆◆

My therapist told me to use some imagination while making love with my husband.

I said, 'You mean imagine it's good?'

What's the difference between 'Oooh!' and 'Aaah!'?

About three inches.

Husband:

Let's go out and have some fun tonight.

Wife:

OK, but if you get home before I do, leave the front door unlocked.

**

A woman was asked in a survey how she felt about condoms. She said, 'Depends on what's in it for me.'

**

My ex-husband has ESP —
Extremely Small Penis.

* * *

Why does an elephant have
4 feet?

Because 8 inches just
isn't enough.

* * *

What's the difference
between a whale and a
husband?

A whale mates for life.

Husband:

Dear, I have some good news and some bad news. First, I'm going to run off with Jane.

Wife:

Really, and what's the bad news?

Husband:

Honey, has the paperboy come yet?

Wife:

No, but he's breathing hard.

◍◍◍

It's a miracle!' the man shouted, waking up his wife.

When I went to the bathroom just now the light came on — even though I hadn't touched the switch. Then, when I was finished, the light went off all by itself! It's a miracle!'

It's not a miracle,' his wife replied. 'You just pissed in the refrigerator again.'

◍◍◍

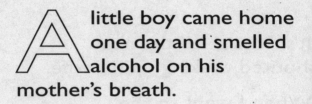A little boy came home one day and smelled alcohol on his mother's breath.

'Mummy,' he said, 'You're wearing Daddy's perfume!'

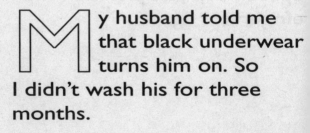My husband told me that black underwear turns him on. So I didn't wash his for three months.

1st Woman:

Do you know, for 25 years
my husband and I were
deliriously happy.

2nd Woman:

Then what happened?

1st Woman:

We met.

When a man and a
woman marry
they become one.
The trouble starts when they
try to decide which one.

My husband brought home a big tube of KY jelly and told me it would make me a happy woman. He was right. When he went out of the bedroom I put some on the doorknob, closed the door and he couldn't get back in.

Mummy, Dad's on his feet again.'

'Shut up and reload.'

At the funeral a close friend said to the widow,

'You won't find another man like him.'

The widow replied,

'Who's gonna look?'

◆◆◆

A little girl came running into the house and said,

  'Mummy, Mummy, can little girls have babies?'

  'No, of course not,' replied her mother.

The little girl ran outside again and shouted,

  'It's OK boys, we can play that game again!'

◆◆◆

How is sex better than bowling?

The balls are lighter and you don't have to change your shoes.

– **|** –

When does a woman stop masturbating?

After the divorce.

– **|** –

How do you get your husband out of a tree?

Cut the rope.

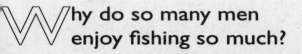hy do so many men enjoy fishing so much?

Because it's the only time anyone says to them, 'Wow! That's a big one.'

After four drinks my husband turns into an animal.

After five I usually pass out.

My husband said that his doctor needed a urine specimen, a stool sample and a semen specimen.
I told him 'Just give him your underwear.'

How are penises like fish?

The little ones you throw back. The big ones you mount.

What's a man's idea of hard work?

A buttoned corset.

What do you call a man who reads the *Sunday Sport*?

An intellectual.

Two women at a rugby match, the first woman shouted,

'Great tackle.'

'Yes,' said the other, 'and a great bum too.'

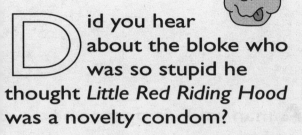

Did you hear about the bloke who was so stupid he thought *Little Red Riding Hood* was a novelty condom?

Where do men usually go to meet their friends?

The VD clinic.

A man told his doctor he could only achieve climax in the doggie position.

'What's wrong with that?' said the doctor.

'The dog's got bad breath.'

***

Wife:

Fancy trying something from the *Kama Sutra*?

Husband:

No, I don't like Indian food.

What's the difference between my boyfriend and a football player?

They both dribble when they're trying to score.

What's the similarity between sex with a man and a Hepatitis B injection?

A quick, short prick in the backside and it's finished.

How are men like old age?

They both come too soon.

What's a man's idea of foreplay?

'You awake?'

How do you know when a man has had an orgasm?

You can hear him snoring.

What's the difference between sex with a man and an Opal Fruit?

Men can't come in four refreshing fruit flavours.

– 1 –

What's the difference between a man's willy and an ice-lolly?

An ice-lolly doesn't mind if you bite a bit off and chew on it.

How is my husband like a deadly cobra?

No one in their right mind would get into bed with either of them.

What do most men say when told that during sex 100 per cent of men have an orgasm compared to only 4 per cent of women?

Who cares?

How are men like stamps?

One lick and they'll stick to you.

How are men like dogs?

One stroke and they'll follow you.

How are men like riding stables?

Both are either vacant or full of shit.

Why do men like being legless?

It's the only time they can boast that their willies touch the floor.

Why is Guy Fawkes such a
hero to men?

Because he had a limp
fuse when it came
to a blow job.

What's the difference
between a man and a
cucumber?

A cucumber stays hard
for longer.

How is a willy like a woman with a broken leg?

They both have difficulty standing up.

- 1 -

What's the difference between a man and concrete?

Concrete eventually gets hard.

What's the definition of
boxer shorts?

Fallout.

Which four letter words
offend men?

Don't and Stop.

What's a man's favourite
food?

Crumpet.

How are hopeless men
like Herpes?

You can't get rid of either
of them once you've
got them.

What's the difference
between a man and
a condom?

Condoms are no longer thick
and insensitive.

What is a man's idea of oral contraception?

Talking your way out of it.

How are men like condoms?

They come in three sizes, small, medium and liar.

Why don't men suffer from haemorrhoids?

Because they're such perfect arseholes.

◄ ♦ ►

Why do men eat vegetables?

To increase their IQ's.

◄ ♦ ►

What's a man's idea of serious commitment?

'OK, I'll stay the night.'